Birds of Presidents

Grace Hansen

Abdo Kids Junior
is an Imprint of Abdo Kids
abdobooks.com

PETS OF PRESIDENTS

abdobooks.com

Published by Abdo Kids, a division of ABDO, P.O. Box 398166, Minneapolis, Minnesota 55439. Copyright © 2022 by Abdo Consulting Group, Inc. International copyrights reserved in all countries. No part of this book may be reproduced in any form without written permission from the publisher. Abdo Kids Junior™ is a trademark and logo of Abdo Kids.

Printed in the United States of America, North Mankato, Minnesota.

102021

012022

 THIS BOOK CONTAINS RECYCLED MATERIALS

Photo Credits: Library of Congress, Shutterstock, ©Thomas Jefferson Foundation at Monticello p9

Production Contributors: Teddy Borth, Jennie Forsberg, Grace Hansen

Design Contributors: Candice Keimig, Pakou Moua

Library of Congress Control Number: 2021939930

Publisher's Cataloging-in-Publication Data

Names: Hansen, Grace, author.

Title: Birds of presidents / by Grace Hansen

Description: Minneapolis, Minnesota : Abdo Kids, 2022 | Series: Pets of presidents | Includes online resources and index.

Identifiers: ISBN 9781098209230 (lib. bdg.) | ISBN 9781644946886 (pbk.) | ISBN 9781098209933 (ebook) | ISBN 9781098260293 (Read-to-Me ebook)

Subjects: LCSH: Birds--Juvenile literature. | Pets--Juvenile literature. | Presidents--Juvenile literature. | Presidents' pets--United States--Juvenile literature.

Classification: DDC 973--dc23

Table of Contents

Birds of Presidents....4

More First Pets......22

Glossary...........23

Index.............24

Abdo Kids Code.....24

Birds of Presidents

Almost every US president has had pets. Some have had birds!

The Washingtons had many birds. Martha loved her green **parrot**!

7

Thomas Jefferson had lots of mockingbirds. One sat on his shoulder while he worked.

The Madisons had a **parrot** named Polly. Polly survived the White House fire of 1814.

The Buchanans had two bald eagles. They were free to fly. But they never went far.

James Buchanan

Rutherford B. Hayes had four canaries. Lucy Hayes loved their singing.

Rutherford and Lucy Hayes

The Roosevelts had a **hyacinth macaw**. Its name was Eli.

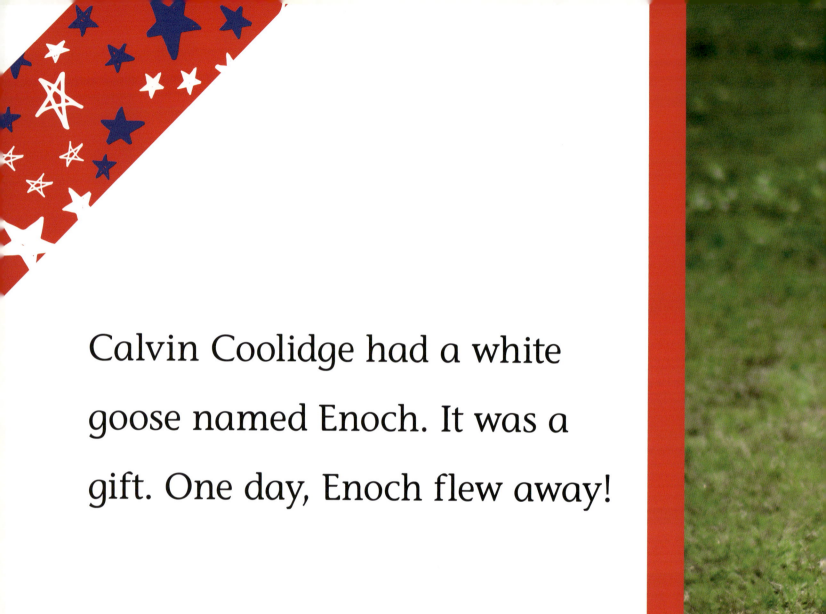

Calvin Coolidge had a white goose named Enoch. It was a gift. One day, Enoch flew away!

LBJ had a pair of lovebirds. He was the last president to have a parrot in the White House.

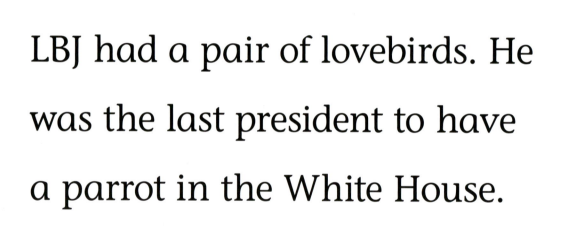

Lyndon B. Johnson

21

More First Pets

Andrew Jackson
Poll • Grey parrot

John Tyler
Johnny Ty • Canary

William McKinley
Washington Post • Yellow-headed amazon

Dwight D. Eisenhower
Gabby • Parakeet

Glossary

hyacinth macaw
a large, brightly colored parrot from central and eastern South America.

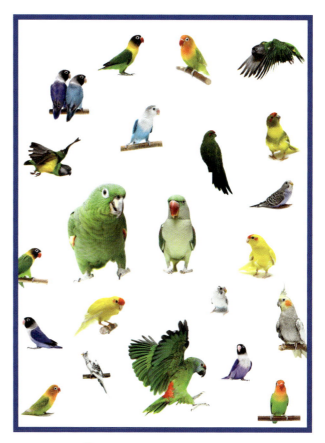

parrot
a tropical bird with a short, hooked bill and, often, brightly colored feathers. There are nearly 400 different kinds of parrots in the world.

Index

bald eagle 12

Buchanans 12

canary 14

Coolidge, Calvin 18

goose 18

Hayes, Rutherford B. 14

hyacinth macaw 16

Jefferson, Thomas 8

Johnson, Lyndon B. 20

lovebird 20

Madisons 10

mockingbirds 8

parrot 6, 10, 16, 20

Roosevelt, Theodore 16

Washingtons 6

Visit **abdokids.com** to access crafts, games, videos, and more!

Use Abdo Kids code **PBK9230** or scan this QR code!